I0816488

MEET SISTER MARY MARGARET

Rebecca W. Martin

Illustrated by

Christopher Tupa

Huntington, Indiana

28 27 26 25 24 23 1 2 3 4 5 6 7 8 9

Our Sunday Visitor Publishing Division
Our Sunday Visitor, Inc.
200 Noll Plaza
Huntington, IN 46750
www.osv.com
1-800-348-2440

ISBN: 978-1-68192-986-6 (Inventory No. T2721)
1. JUVENILE NONFICTION—Religious—Christian—General.
2. JUVENILE NONFICTION—Religious—Christian—Learning Concepts.
3. RELIGION—Christianity—Catholic.

LCCN: 2023934241

Cover and interior design: Lindsey Riesen
Cover and interior art: Christopher Tupa

Printed in Turkey

To the religious women of many orders who have become like family, wherever life takes me. Most especially to my sisters in Saint Dominic, Sister Hyacinth, OP, and Sister Mary Margaret, OP; and my beloved friend Sister Philomena, S. Praem. (RWM)

Hello! How are you?

My name is Sister Mary Margaret. I am a religious sister. Do you know what that means?

As a religious sister, I get to love and serve Jesus in a special way. Instead of getting married, I am a bride of Christ!

I have promised Jesus three things:

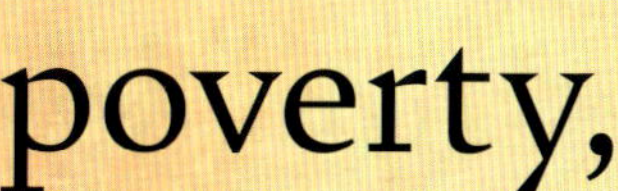

poverty,

chastity,

and obedience.

These are big words!

Poverty means I live simply, like Jesus did. I don't own fancy shoes or a car.

Chastity means that I love Jesus with my whole heart, soul, mind, and body.

Obedience means that I obey the people Jesus puts in charge of me, just like you obey your mom and dad.

These three promises are
called **VOWS.**

As you can see, I dress a little differently from most people. In fact, I wear the same outfit every day. It is called a **habit.**

My habit is like a wedding dress. It tells everyone that I am a bride of Christ.

I have a special name, too. I was given this name when I became a sister. In the Bible, people receive new names when God gives them a mission.

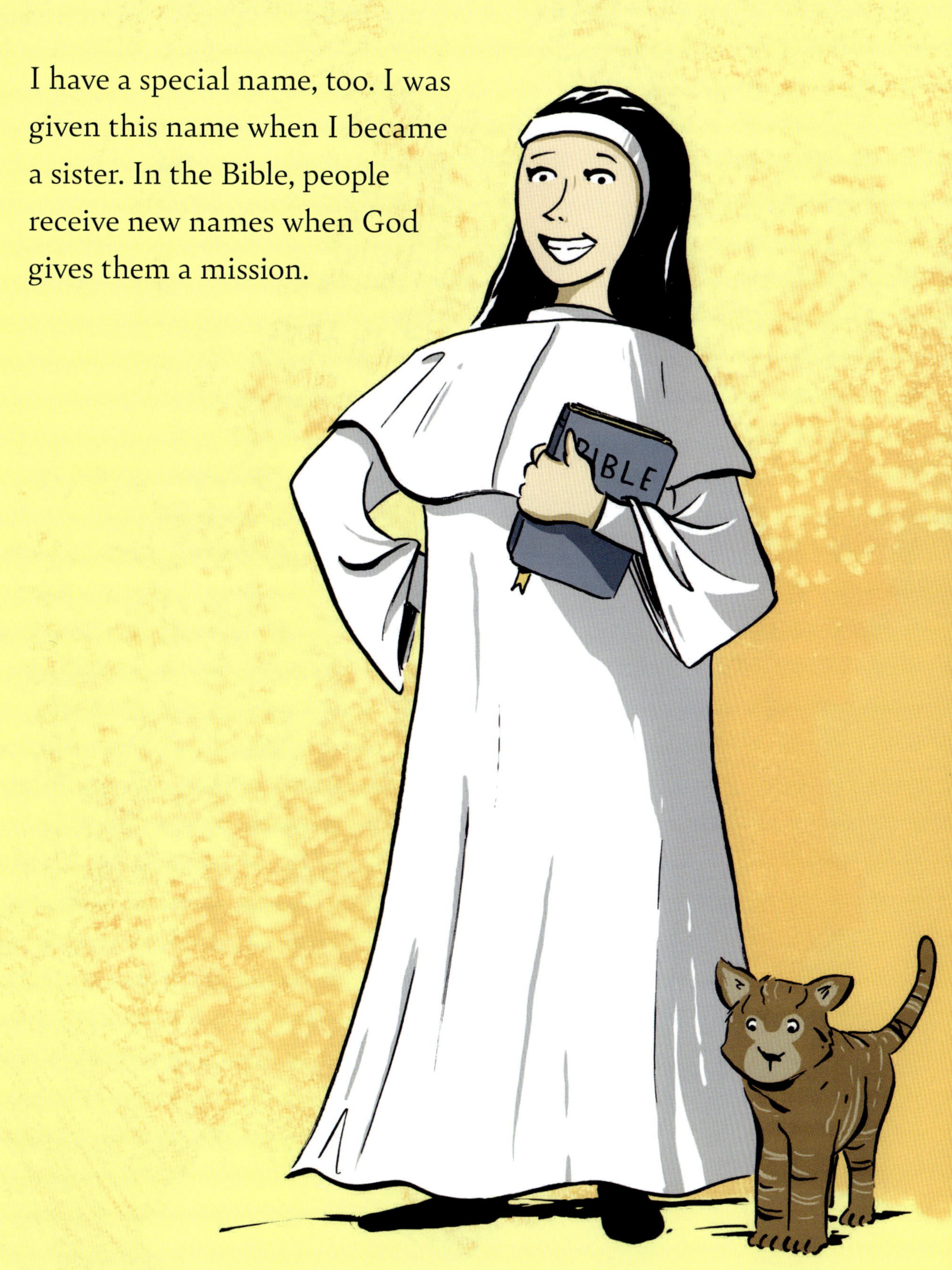

I live in a place called a **convent** with many other religious sisters. We are one big family. Our home is like your home, but bigger!

The convent has a kitchen,

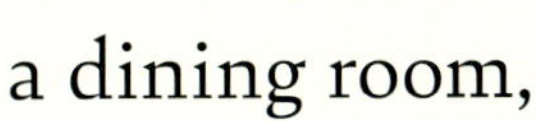

a dining room,

a living room,

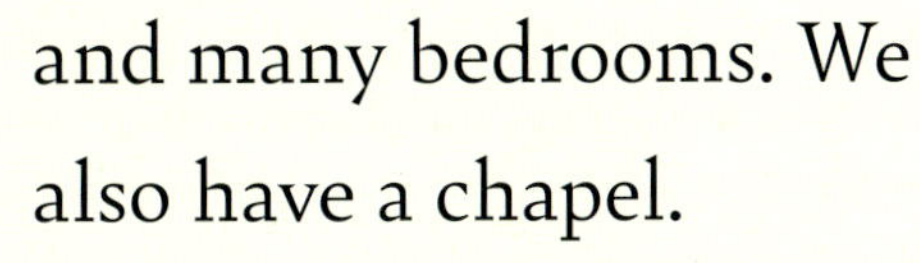

and many bedrooms. We also have a chapel.

Every day, I spend lots of time talking to Jesus. Early in the morning, I go to the chapel to pray. I worship him joyfully in the Mass.

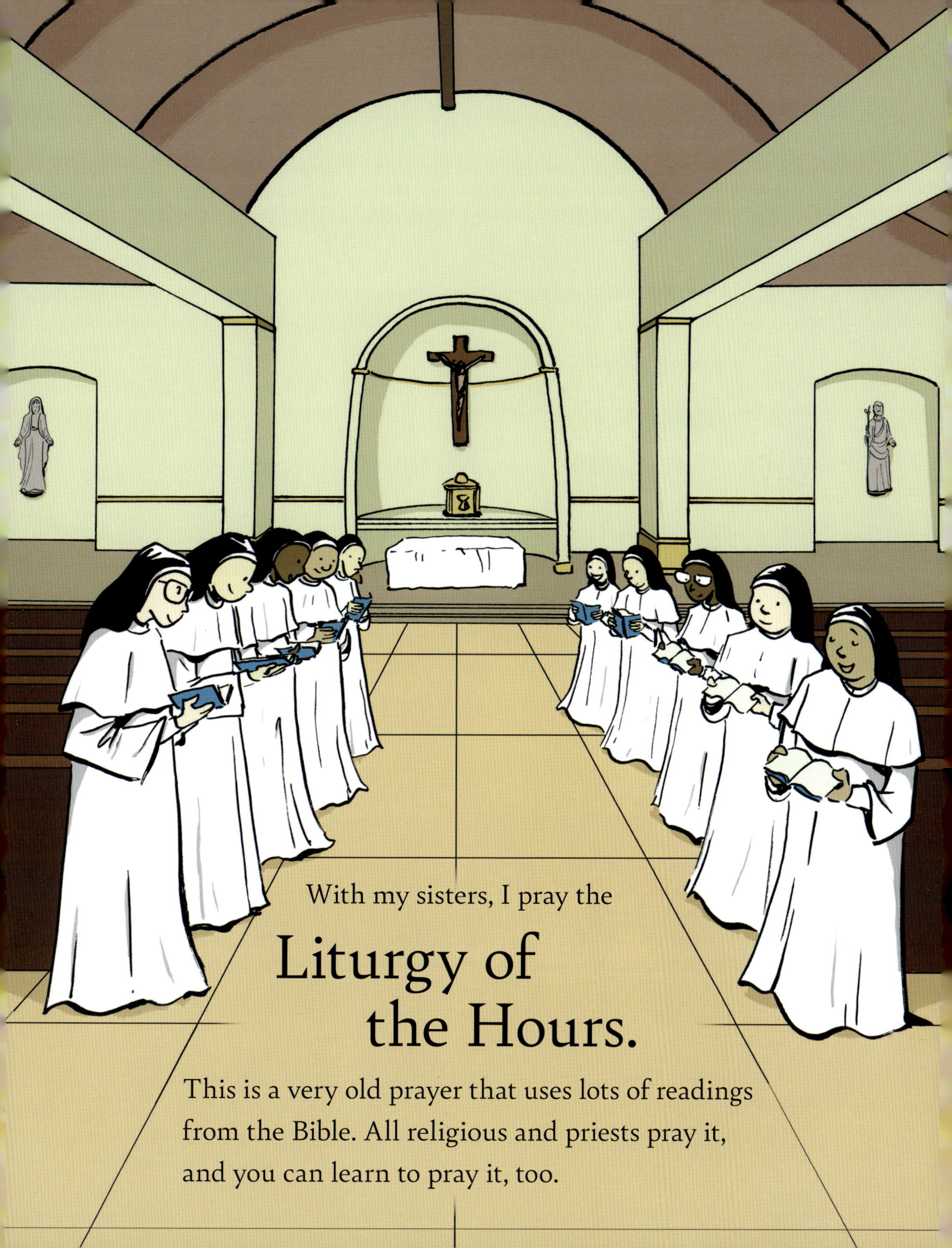

With my sisters, I pray the

Liturgy of the Hours.

This is a very old prayer that uses lots of readings from the Bible. All religious and priests pray it, and you can learn to pray it, too.

After our morning prayers and breakfast, we set out for the day. Each of us has an apostolate. That's another big word. It means the job that each of us does to help the whole Church.

There are many families of religious sisters, and they have different **apostolates.**

Some sisters help sick people.

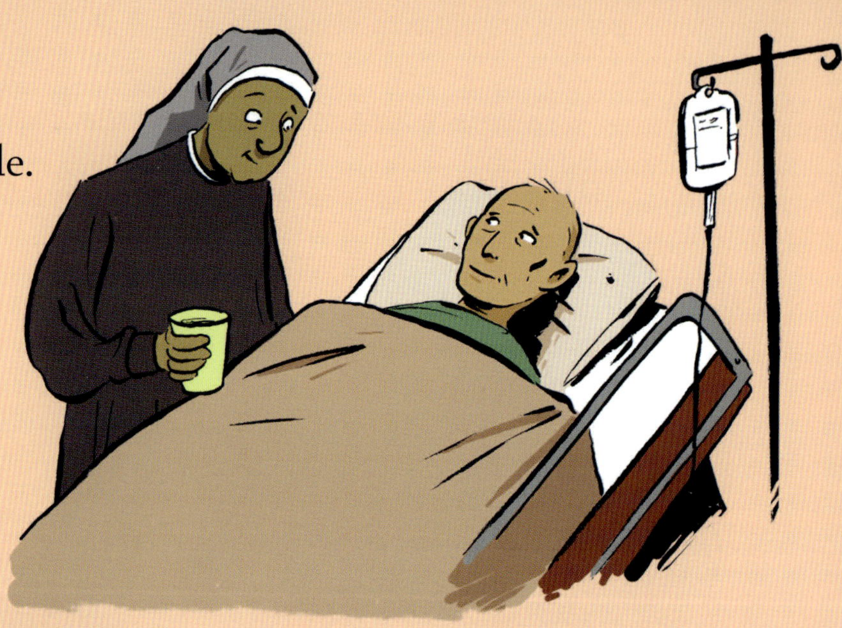

Some sisters are teachers.

Some sisters publish books.

Some sisters care for
mommies and babies.

Some sisters care for
people in need.

Some sisters pray all day long for everyone in the whole world. There are sisters praying for you right now.

At the end of the day, we come home to our convent. We eat dinner together. Sometimes I help cook, and sometimes I help serve the food.

While we eat, one of the sisters reads to us. These books help us learn more about God and how to be **holy.**

I have lots of **fun** with my religious family, just like you do with your family.

After dinner, we play basketball, or put jigsaw puzzles together, or sing songs.

In the winter, we drink hot chocolate and sit near a warm fire!

When it gets late, we go back to the chapel to say goodnight to Jesus.

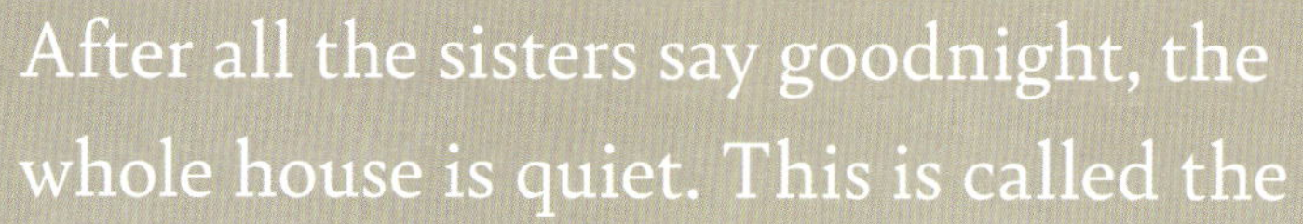

After all the sisters say goodnight, the whole house is quiet. This is called the

Great Silence.

We are quiet so we can listen to Jesus speaking in our hearts. I talk to him about my day and ask him to help me tomorrow.

Now you know a little bit about what it means
to be a **religious sister!**

What do you think God wants you to be when you grow up? How does he want you to love him and other people? Keep listening to your heart and asking Jesus what great plans he has for you!

Dear Jesus,

I love you. Thank you for loving me! Please show me every day how you want me to love you better. As I grow up, show me your will for my life.

Amen.

For Parents

Religious order: a family of religious who all follow the same rule of life and work in the same apostolate

Apostolate: the mission or job that a religious does to serve God and the Church. Women religious pursue many, many apostolates!

Vow: the solemn promise a religious makes to God to live the consecrated life. The vows of poverty, chastity, and obedience are called the "evangelical counsels."

Discernment: the process of praying and listening for God's guidance

Vocation: a state in life in which each person loves God and neighbor in the way his or her heart is formed. This might be marriage, holy orders (for men), consecrated life for men or women, or the single life.

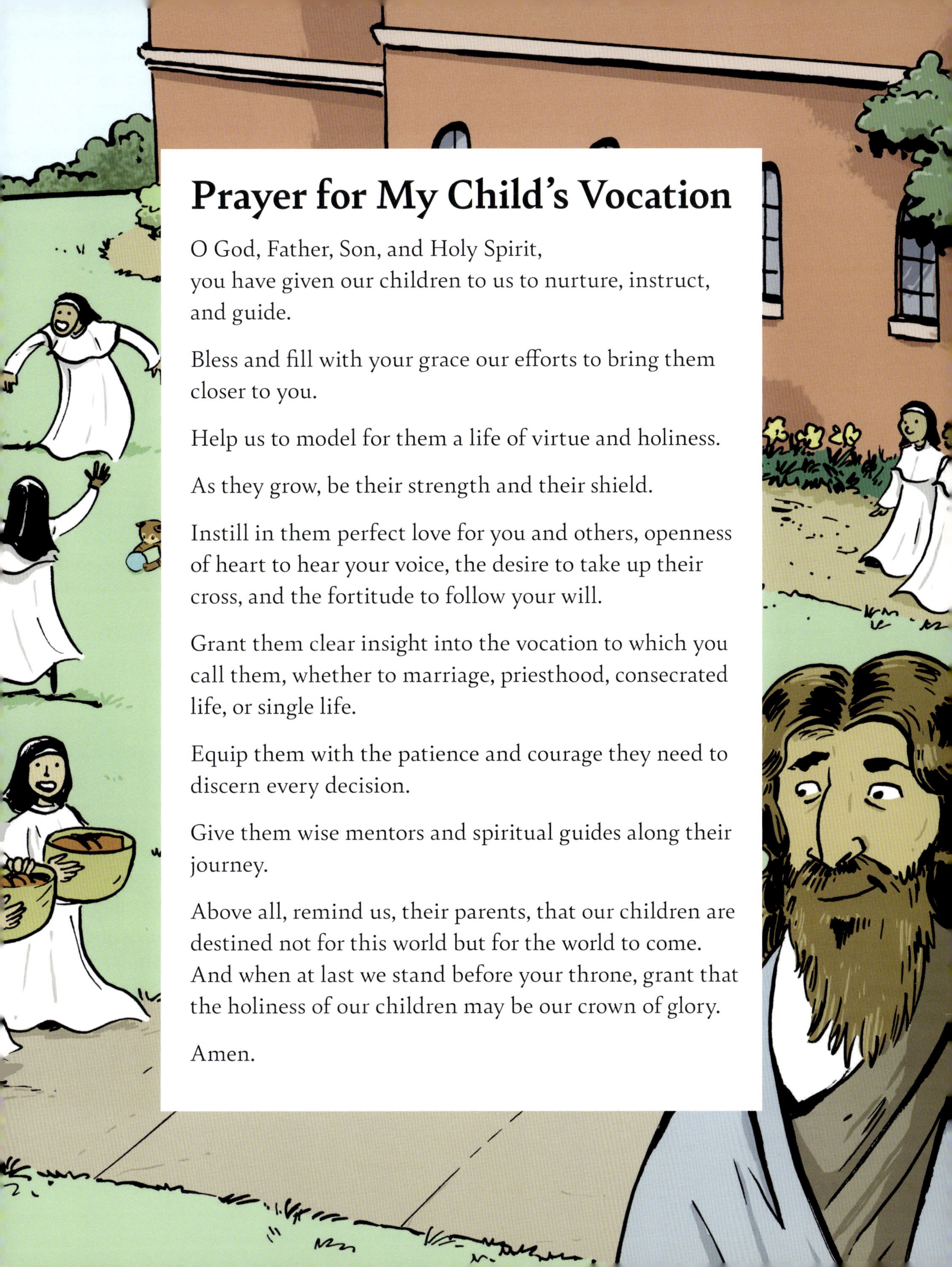

Prayer for My Child's Vocation

O God, Father, Son, and Holy Spirit,
you have given our children to us to nurture, instruct, and guide.

Bless and fill with your grace our efforts to bring them closer to you.

Help us to model for them a life of virtue and holiness.

As they grow, be their strength and their shield.

Instill in them perfect love for you and others, openness of heart to hear your voice, the desire to take up their cross, and the fortitude to follow your will.

Grant them clear insight into the vocation to which you call them, whether to marriage, priesthood, consecrated life, or single life.

Equip them with the patience and courage they need to discern every decision.

Give them wise mentors and spiritual guides along their journey.

Above all, remind us, their parents, that our children are destined not for this world but for the world to come. And when at last we stand before your throne, grant that the holiness of our children may be our crown of glory.

Amen.

Helping families love and live the Catholic Faith

OSV Kids is an exciting new brand on a mission to help children learn about, live, and love the Catholic Faith. Every OSV Kids product is prayerfully developed to introduce children of all ages to Jesus and his Church. Using beautiful artwork, engaging storytelling, and fun activities, OSV Kids products help families form and develop their Catholic identity and learn to live the faith with great joy.

OSV Kids is a monthly magazine that delivers a fun, trustworthy, and faith-filled set of stories, images, and activities designed to help Catholic families with children ages 2-6 build up their domestic churches and live the liturgical year at home.

About the Author

Rebecca W. Martin lives in Michigan with her husband and too many cats. She is an acquisitions editor for Our Sunday Visitor, where she enjoys connecting with authors and developing new books. In 2022, she made her perpetual profession as a Lay Dominican, and serves as editor for *Veritas*, a quarterly Lay Dominican publication. She also freelances with Chrism Press as an assistant fiction editor. Rebecca is an alumna of Christendom College and an active member of the Catholic Writers Guild, and outside of the home office you can usually find her reading, writing, or singing in a concert choir.

About the Illustrator

Christopher Tupa is an artist, book illustrator, and comic creator known for his watercolor work, pop-art aesthetic, and humorous, whimsical style. His illustrations have appeared in books, RPG rule manuals, newpapers, magazines, and on web pages across the globe. Christopher is a big kid at heart who enjoys watching cartoons and playing games when he isn't traveling or exploring the world around him. You can see his work at www.ctupa.com or request commissions through christophertupa@hotmail.com.